Cars Coloring Book For Kids

Coloring Pages for Kids

By Gala Publication

PUBLISHED BY:

Gala Publication

ISBN-13: 978- 1508815860
ISBN-10: 1508815860

©Copyright 2015 – Gala Publication

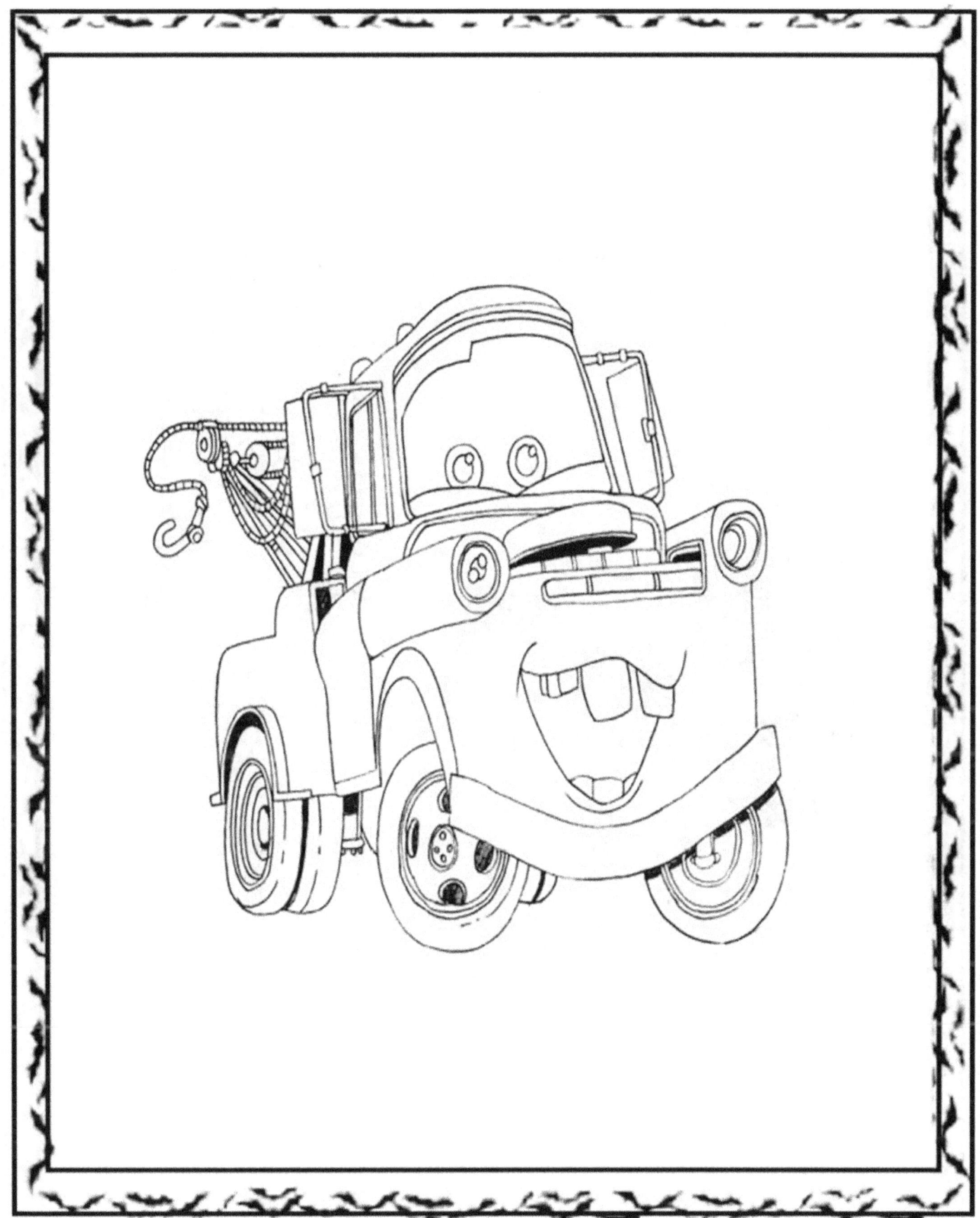

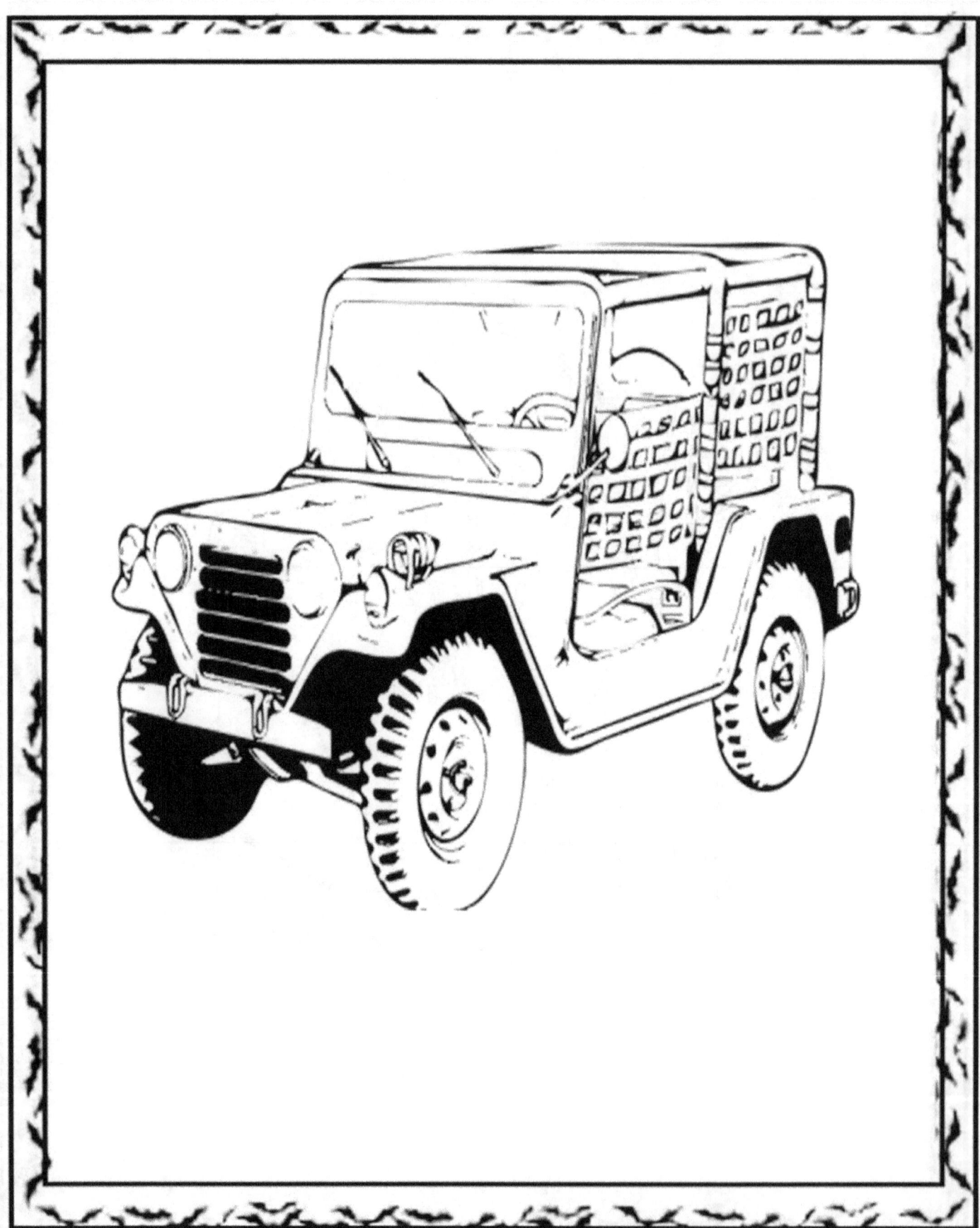

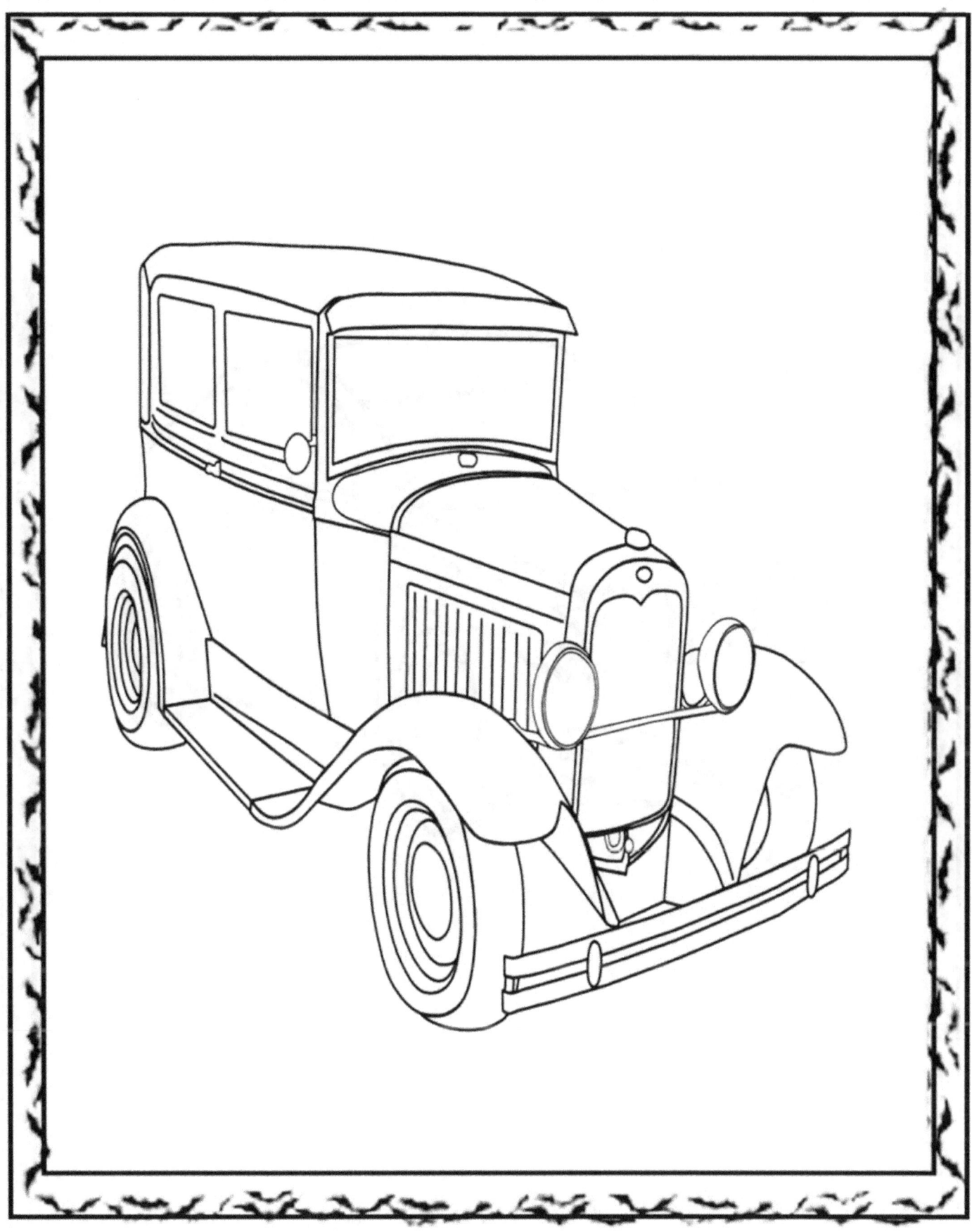

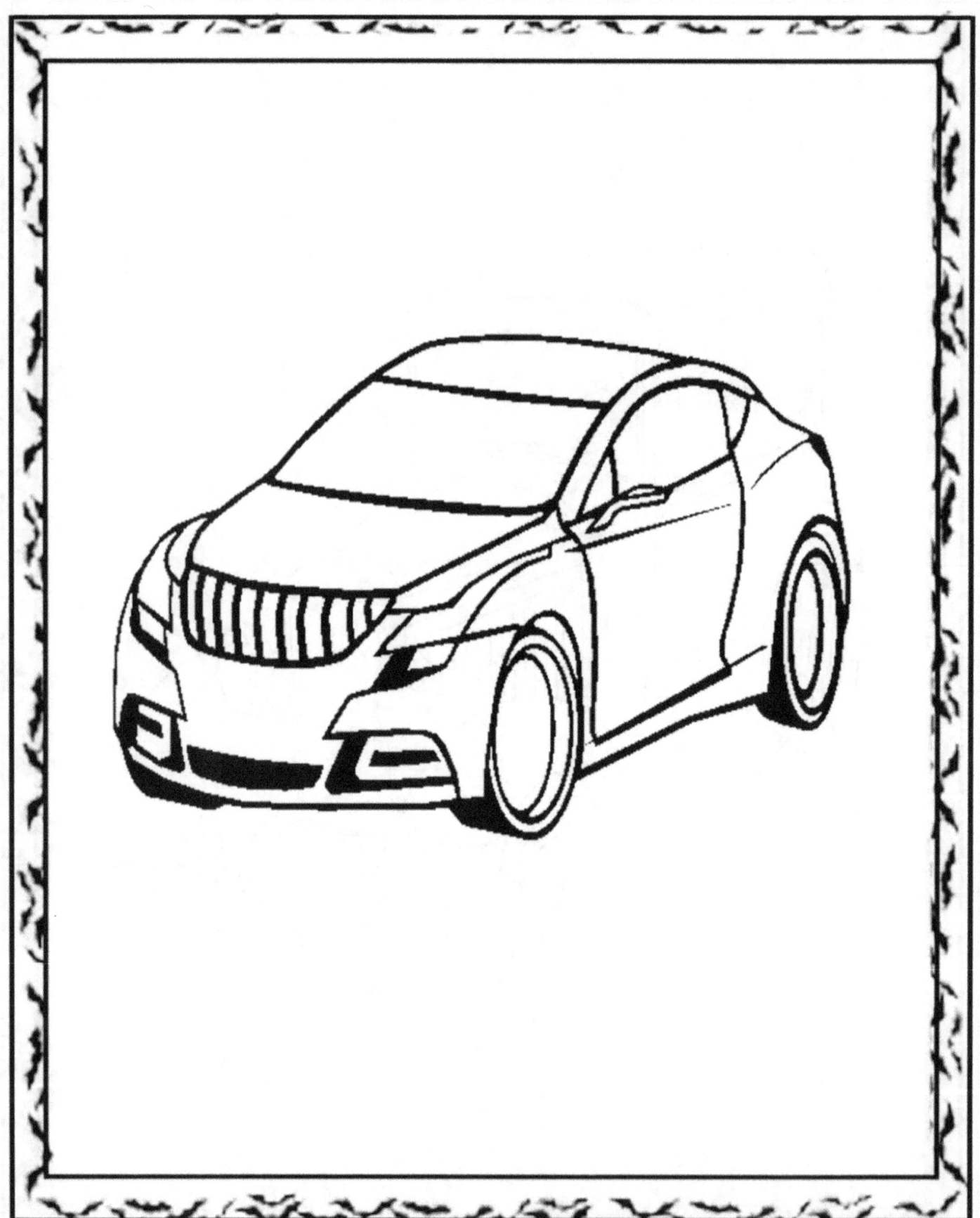

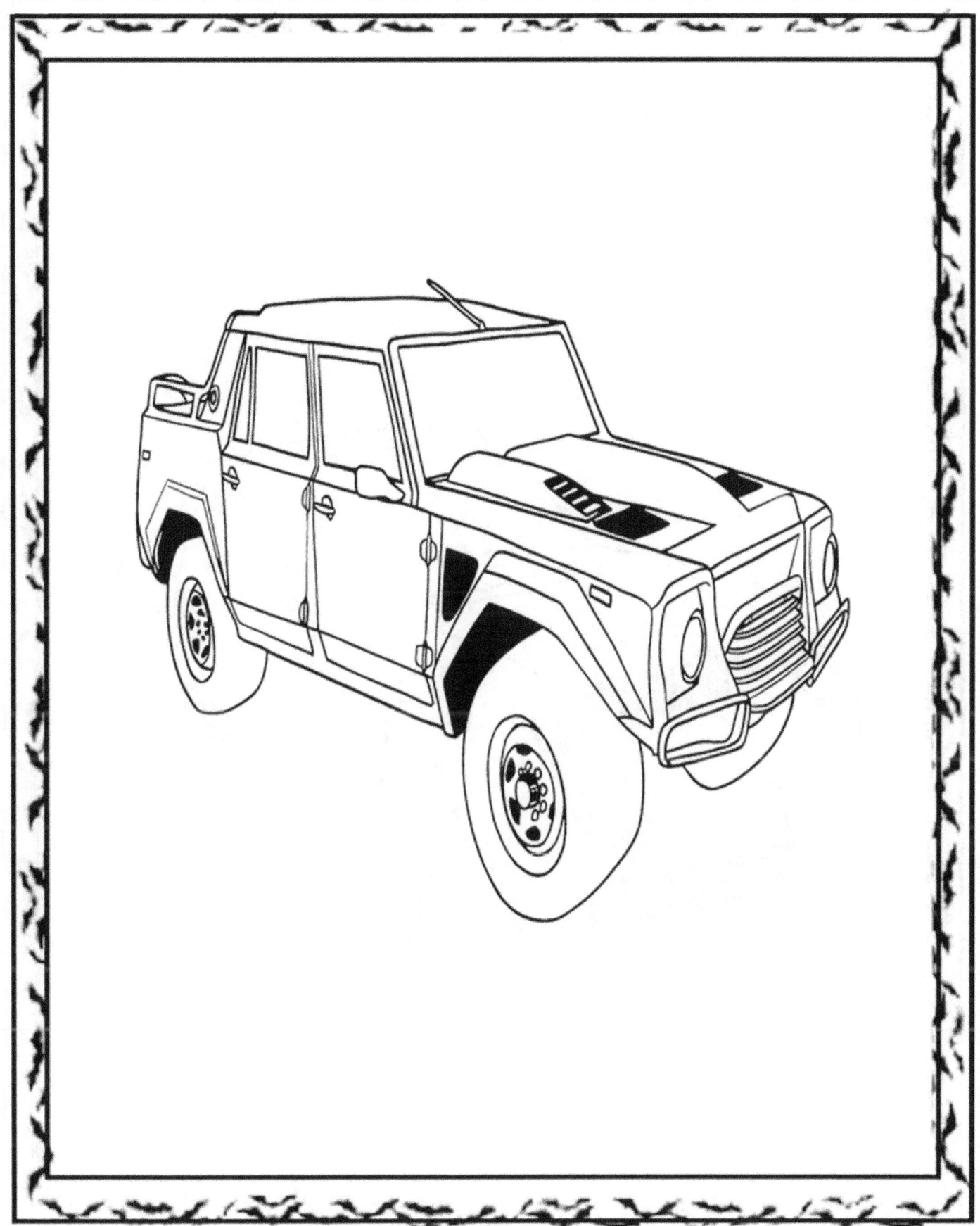

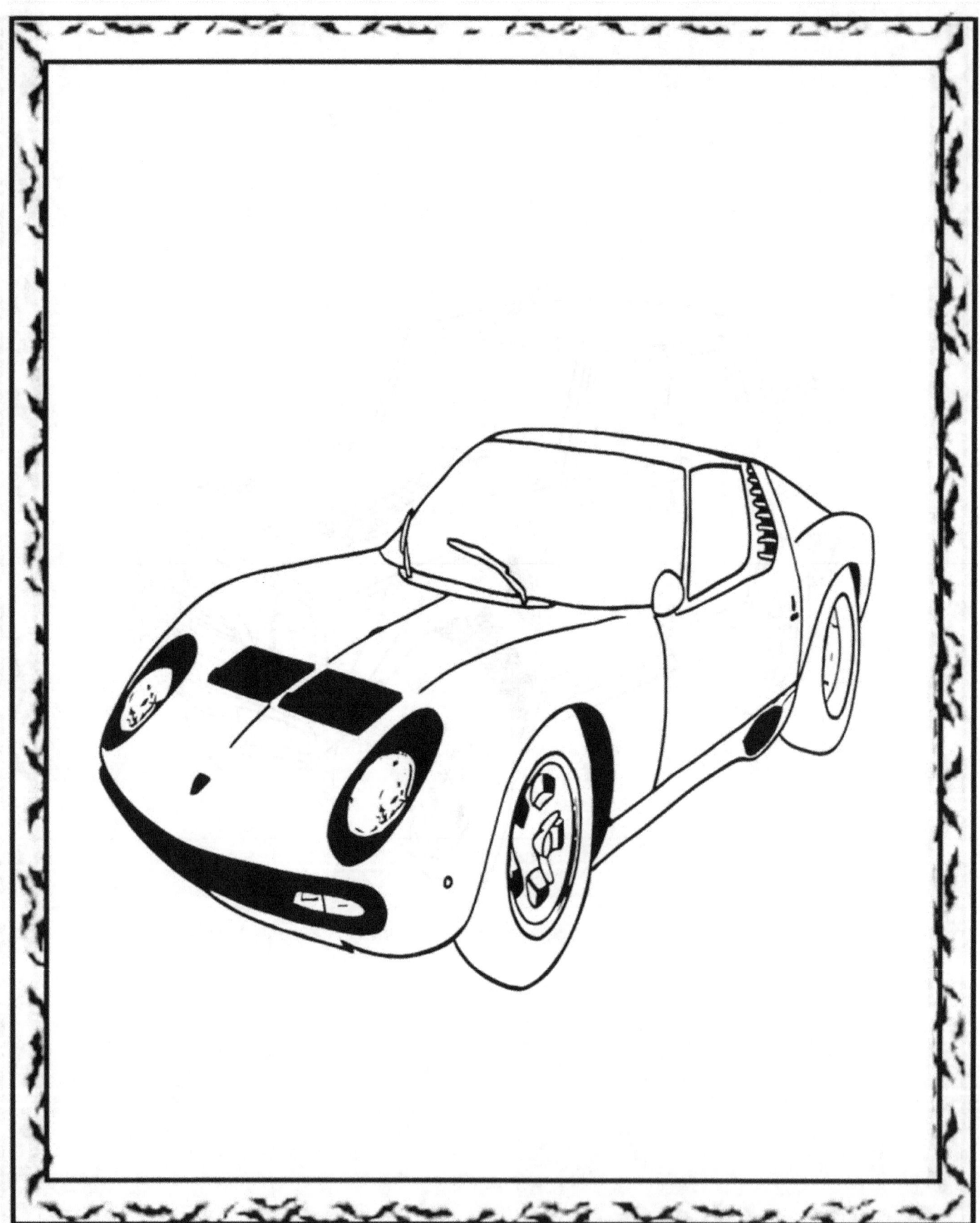

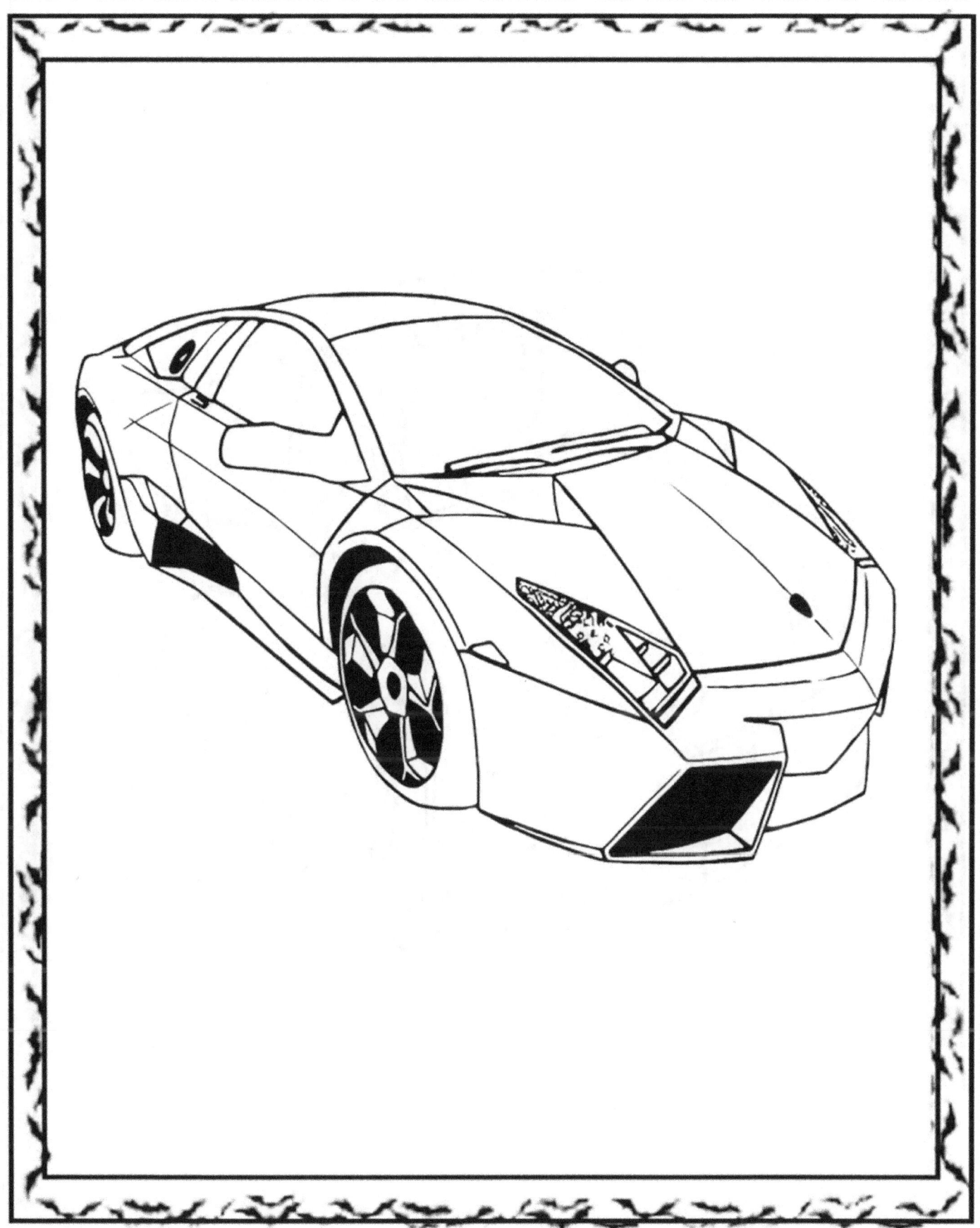

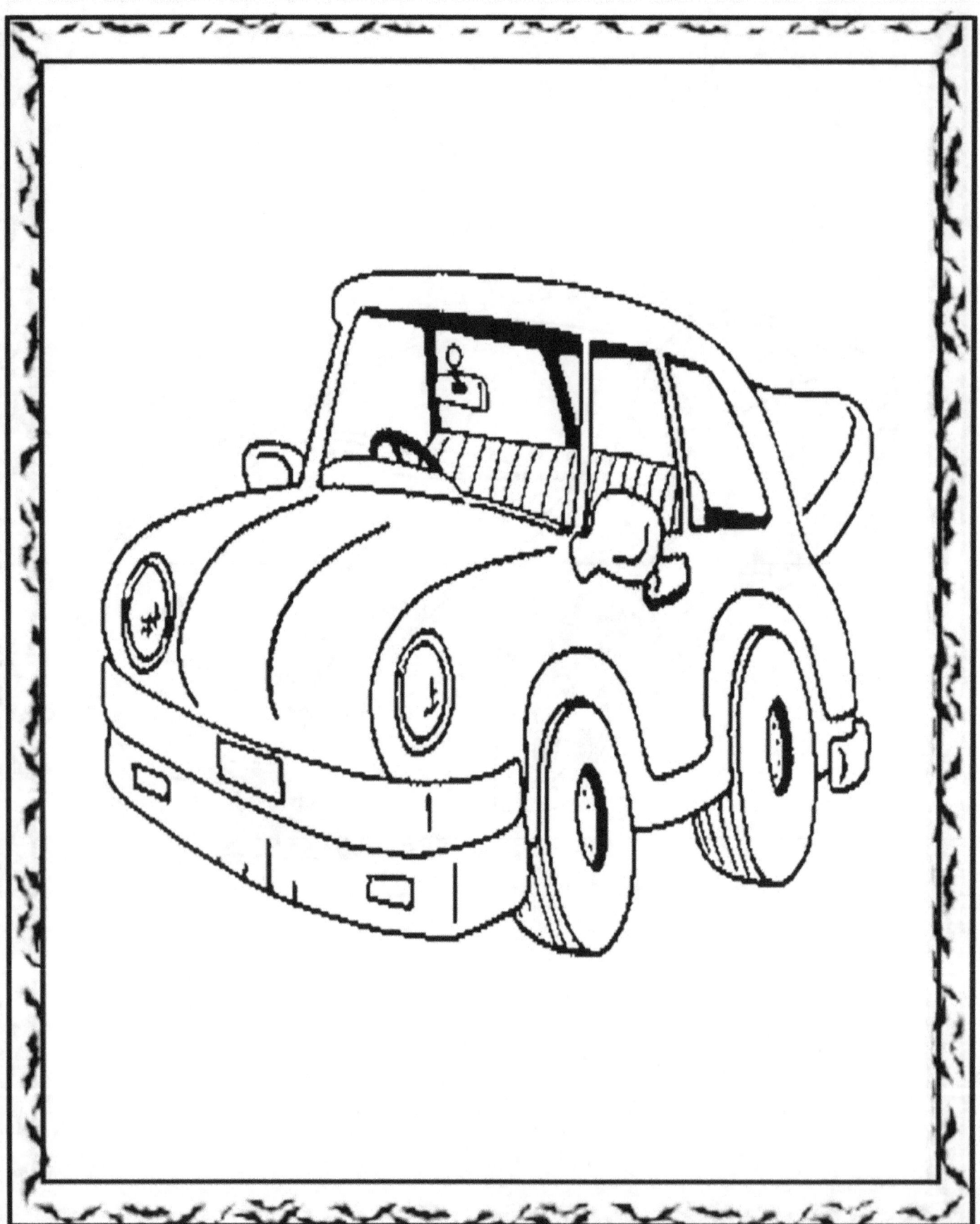

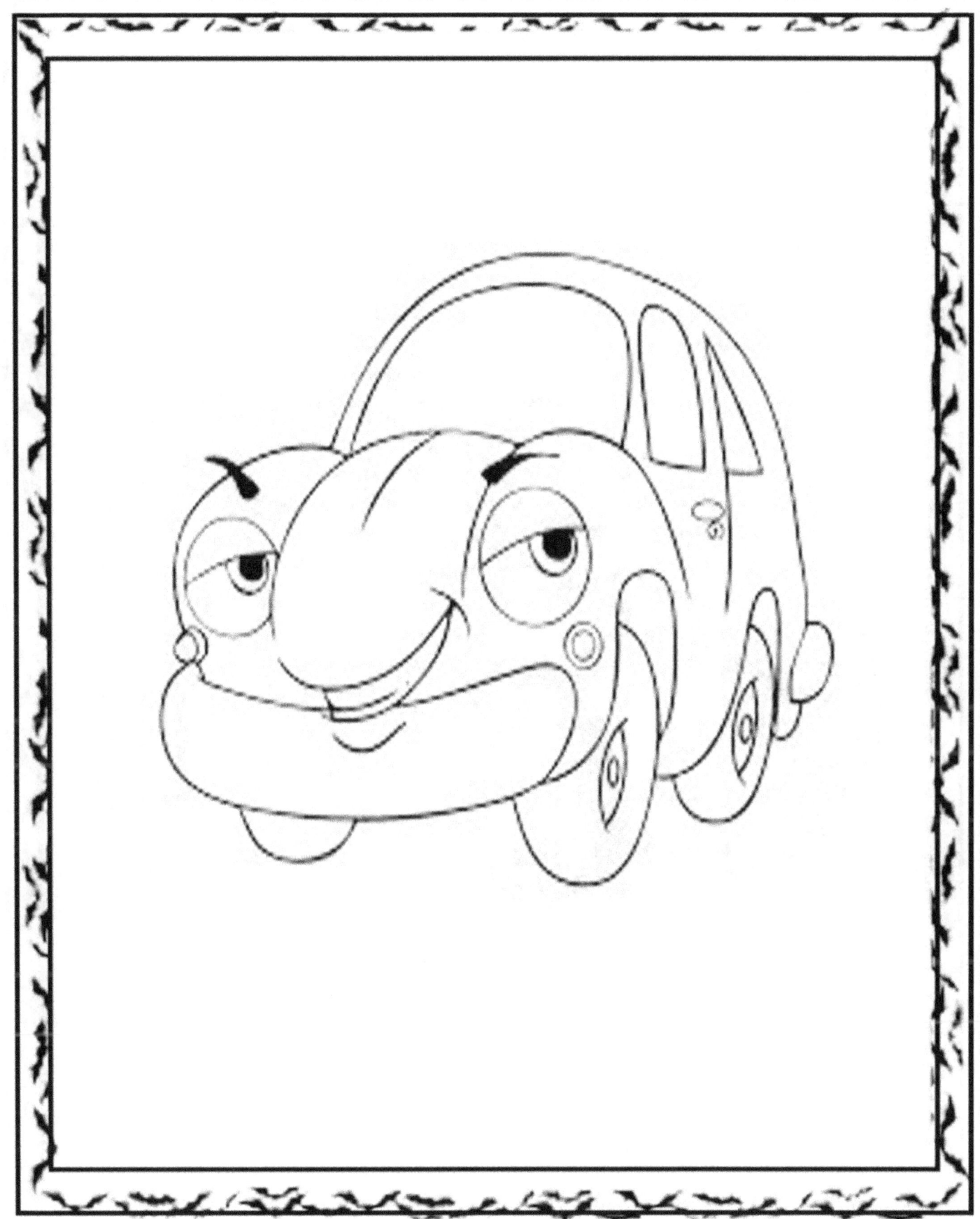

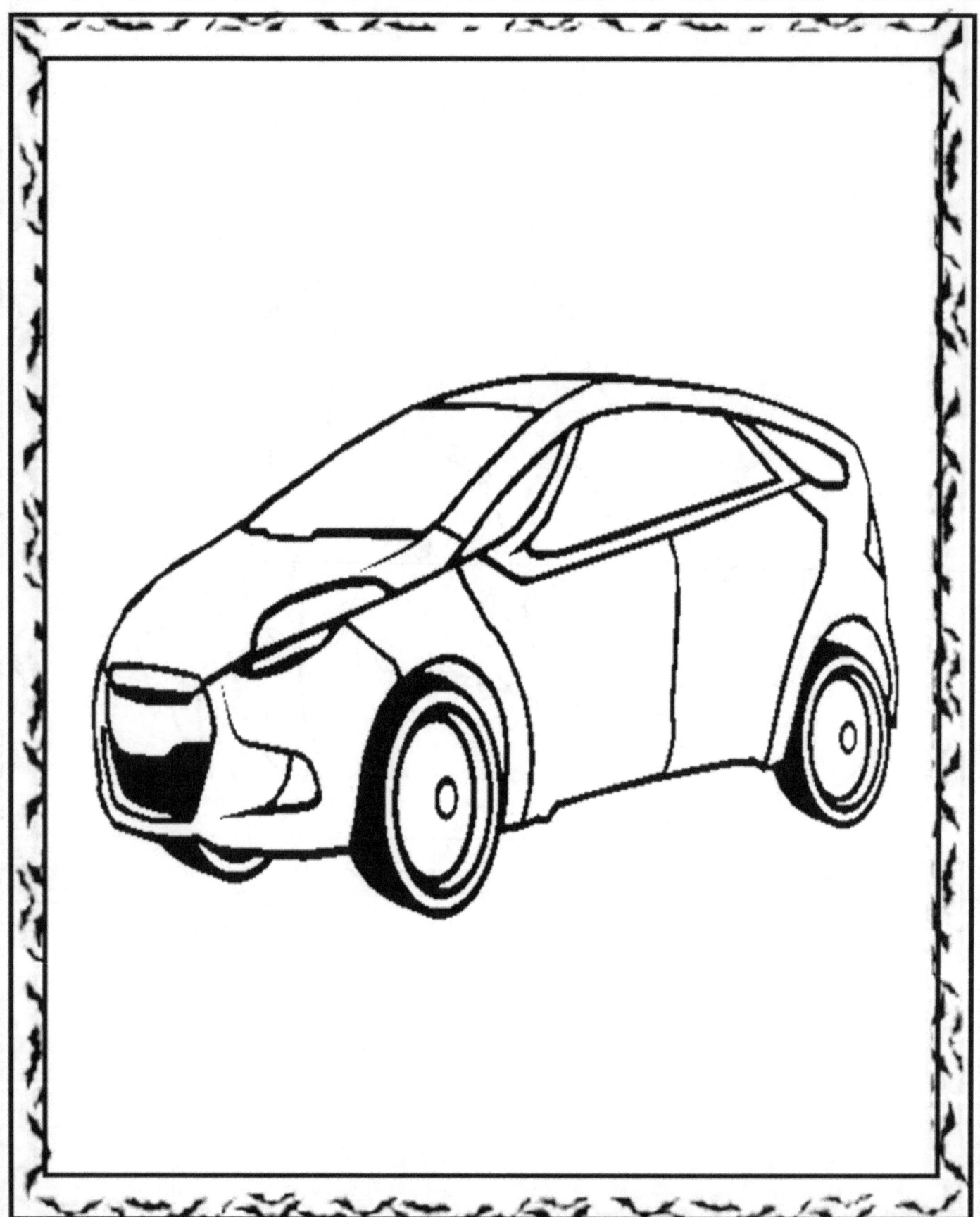

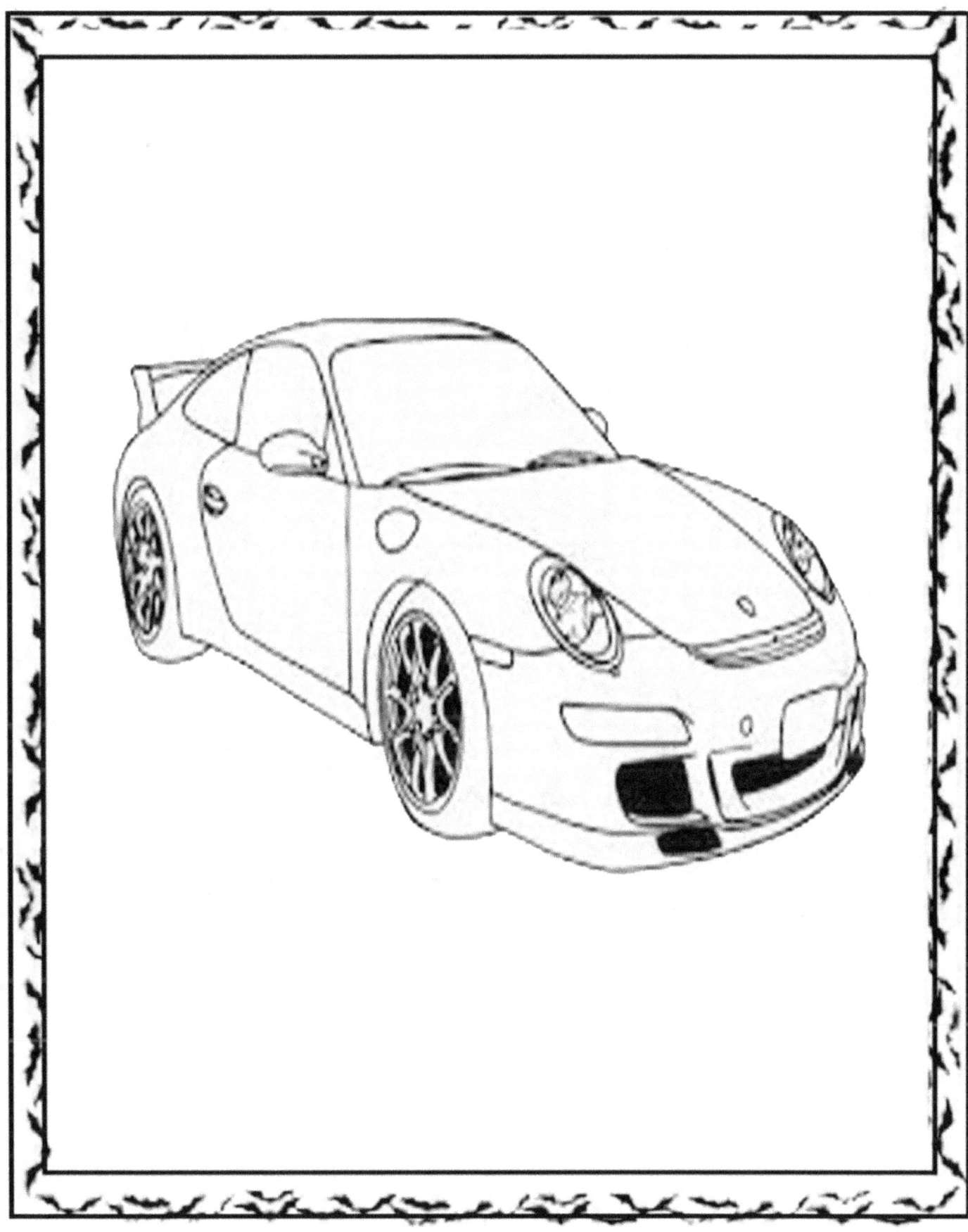

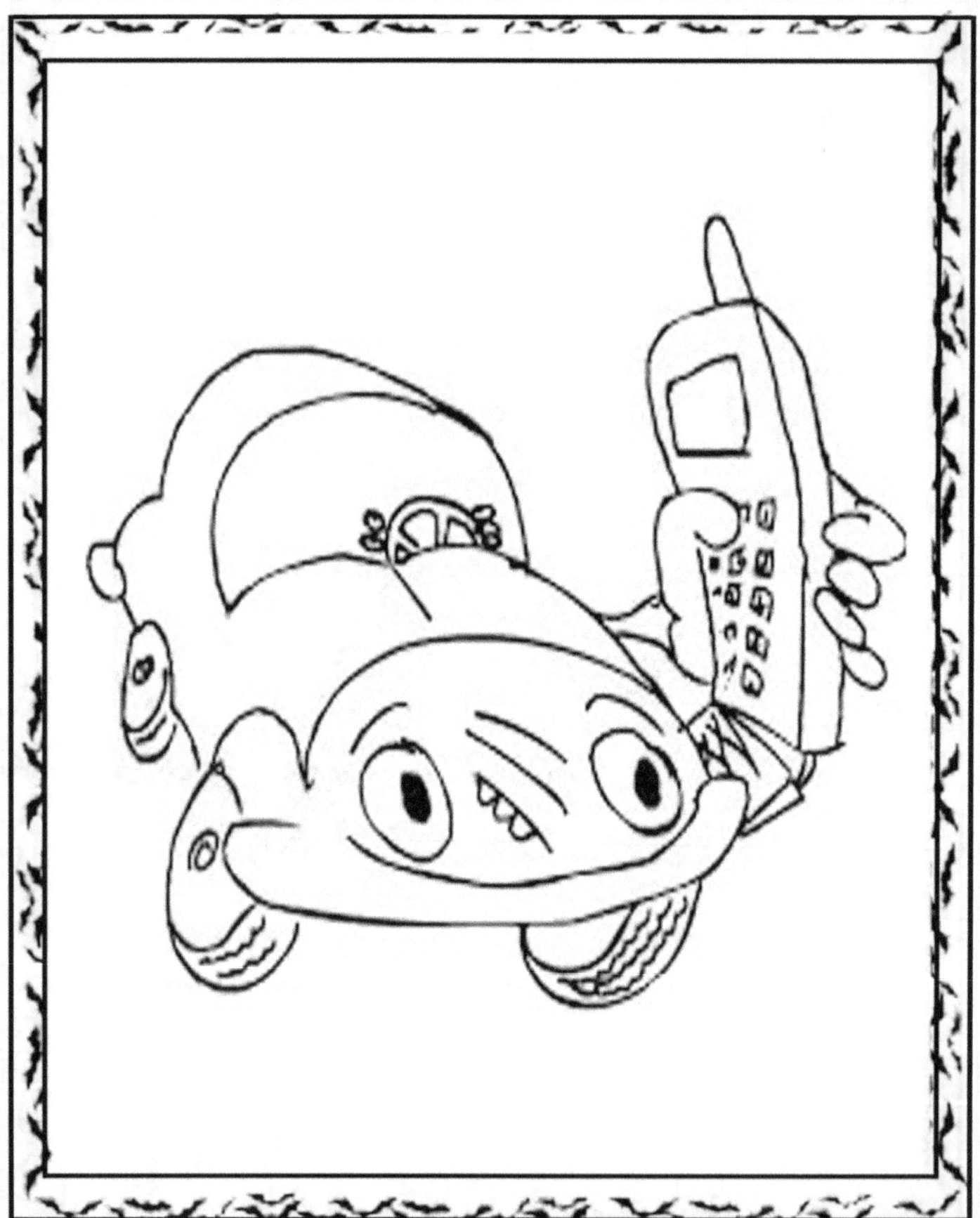

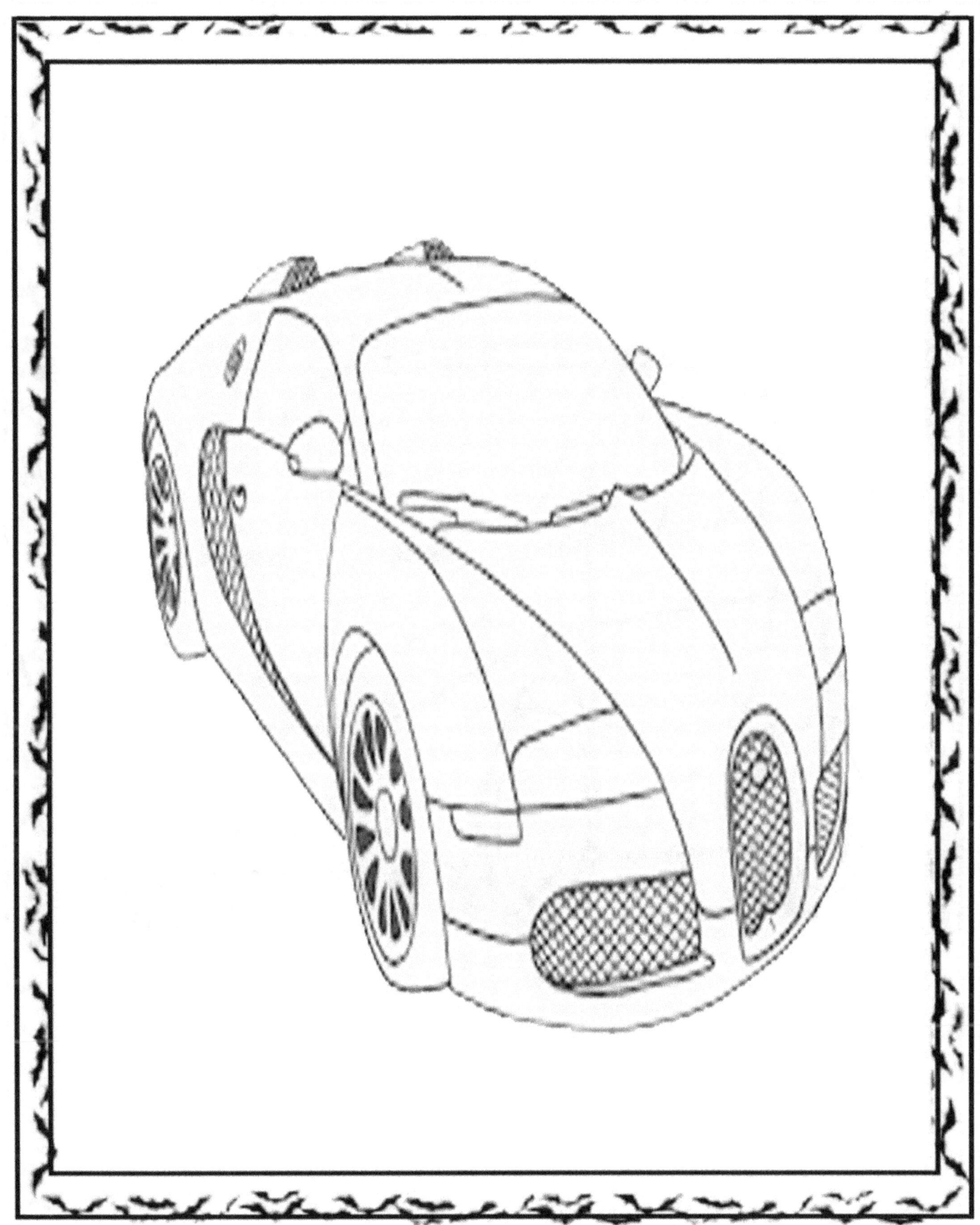

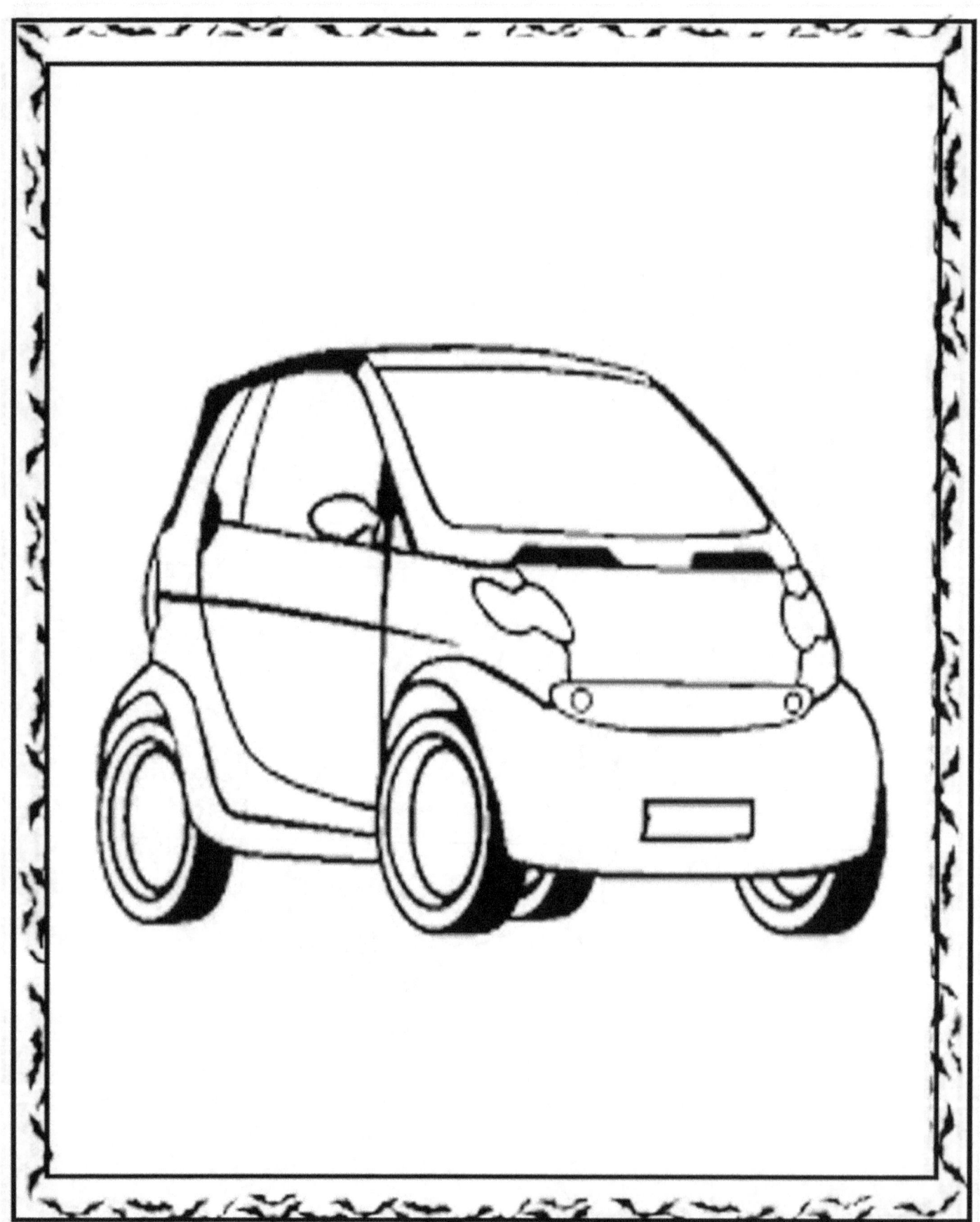

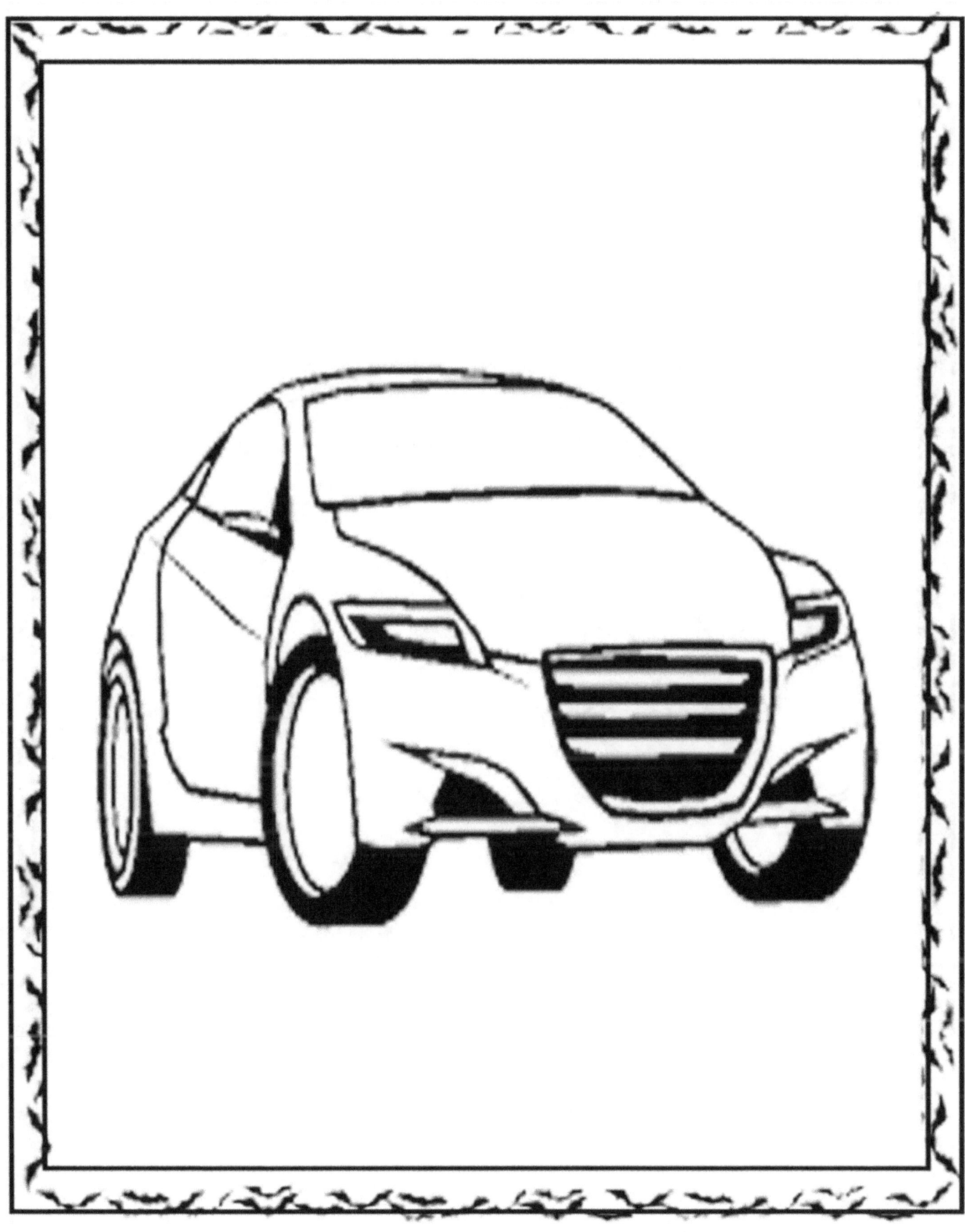

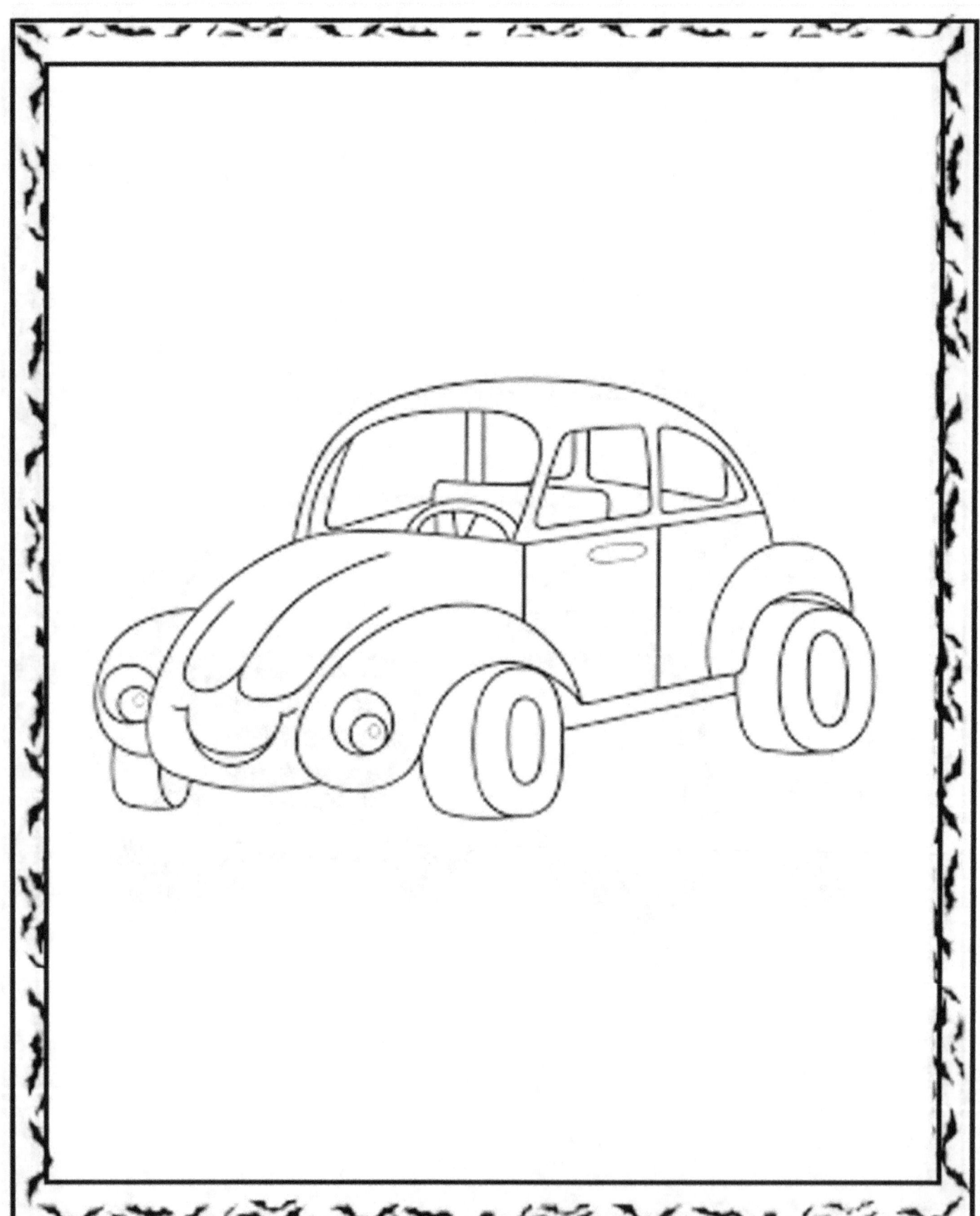

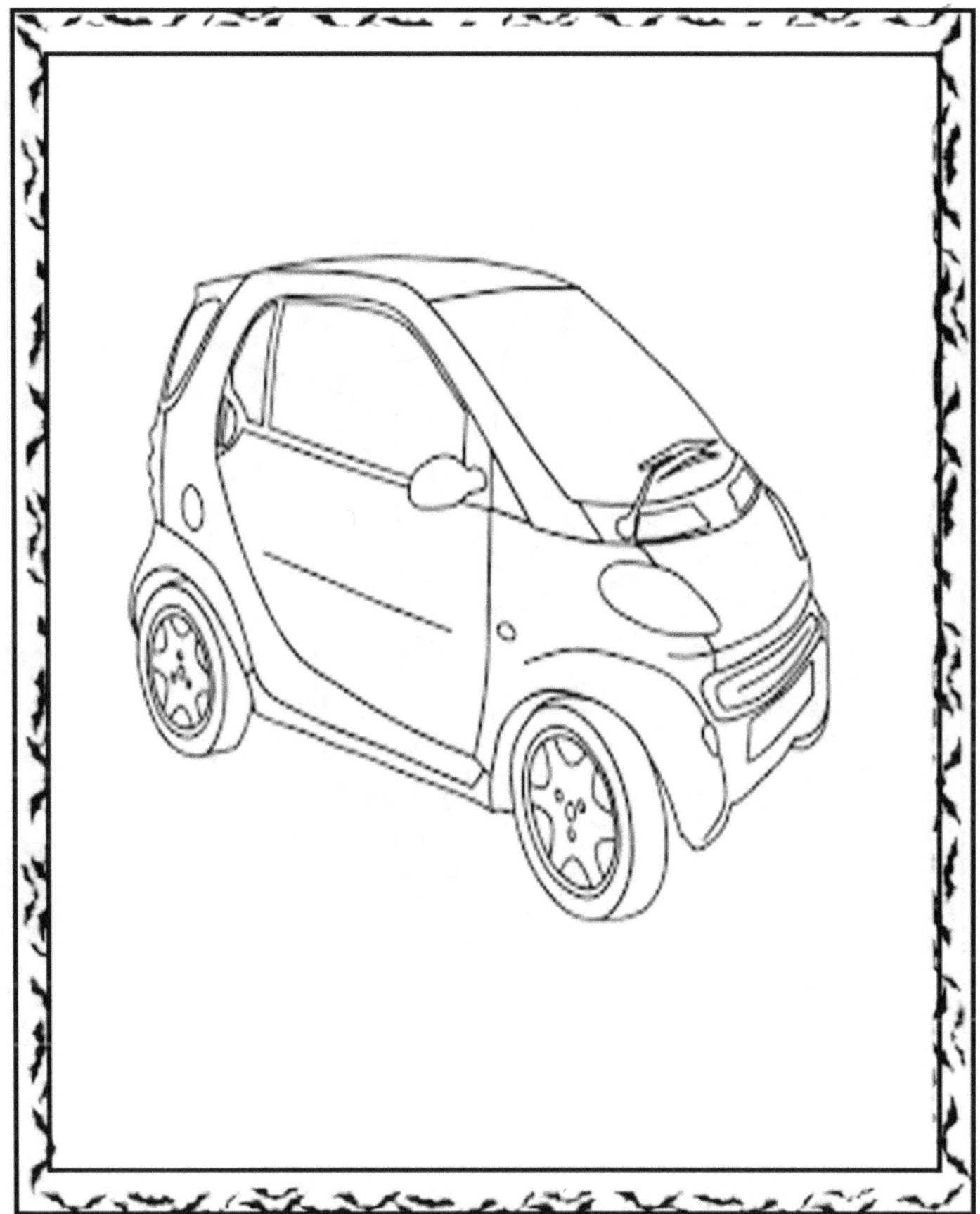

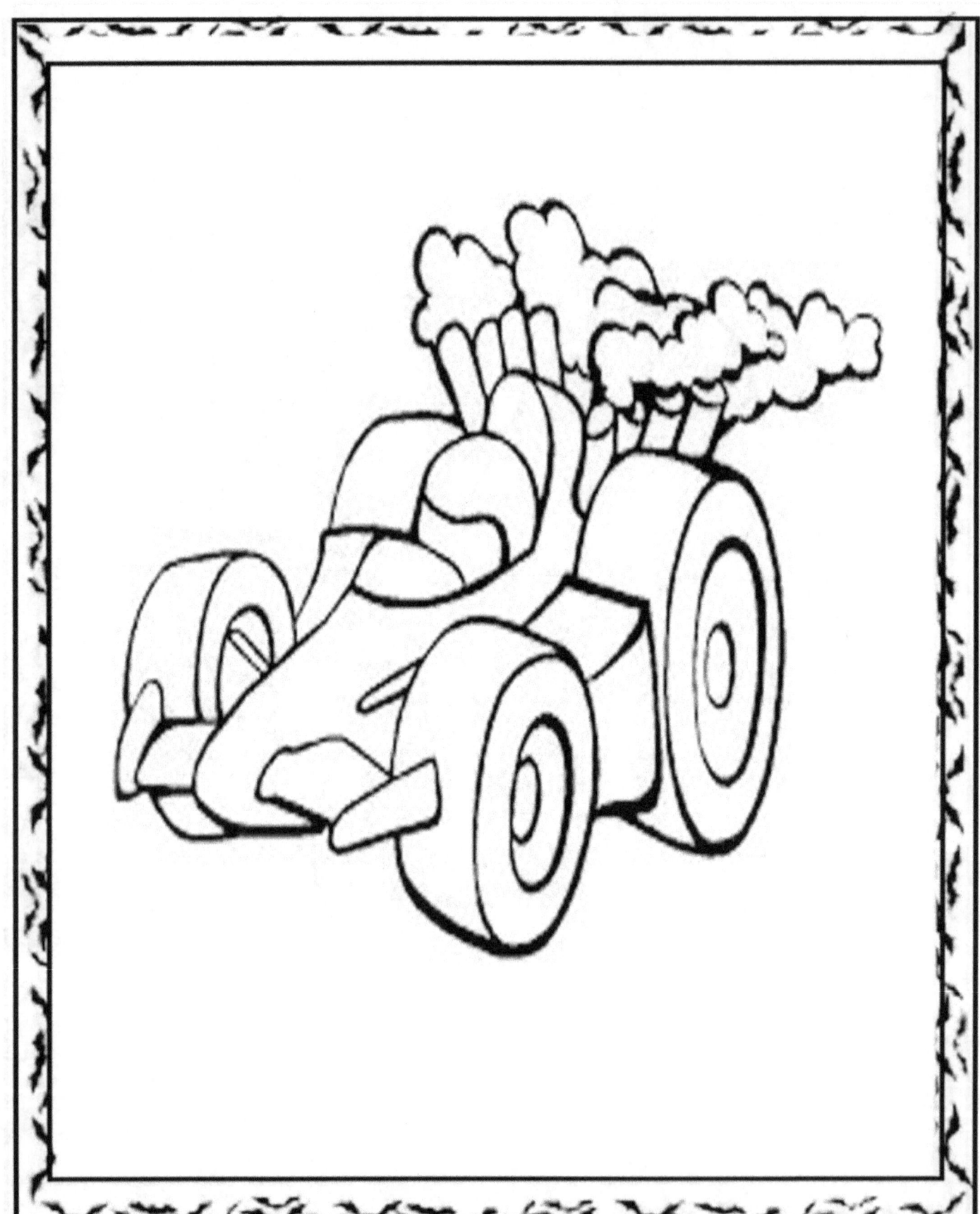

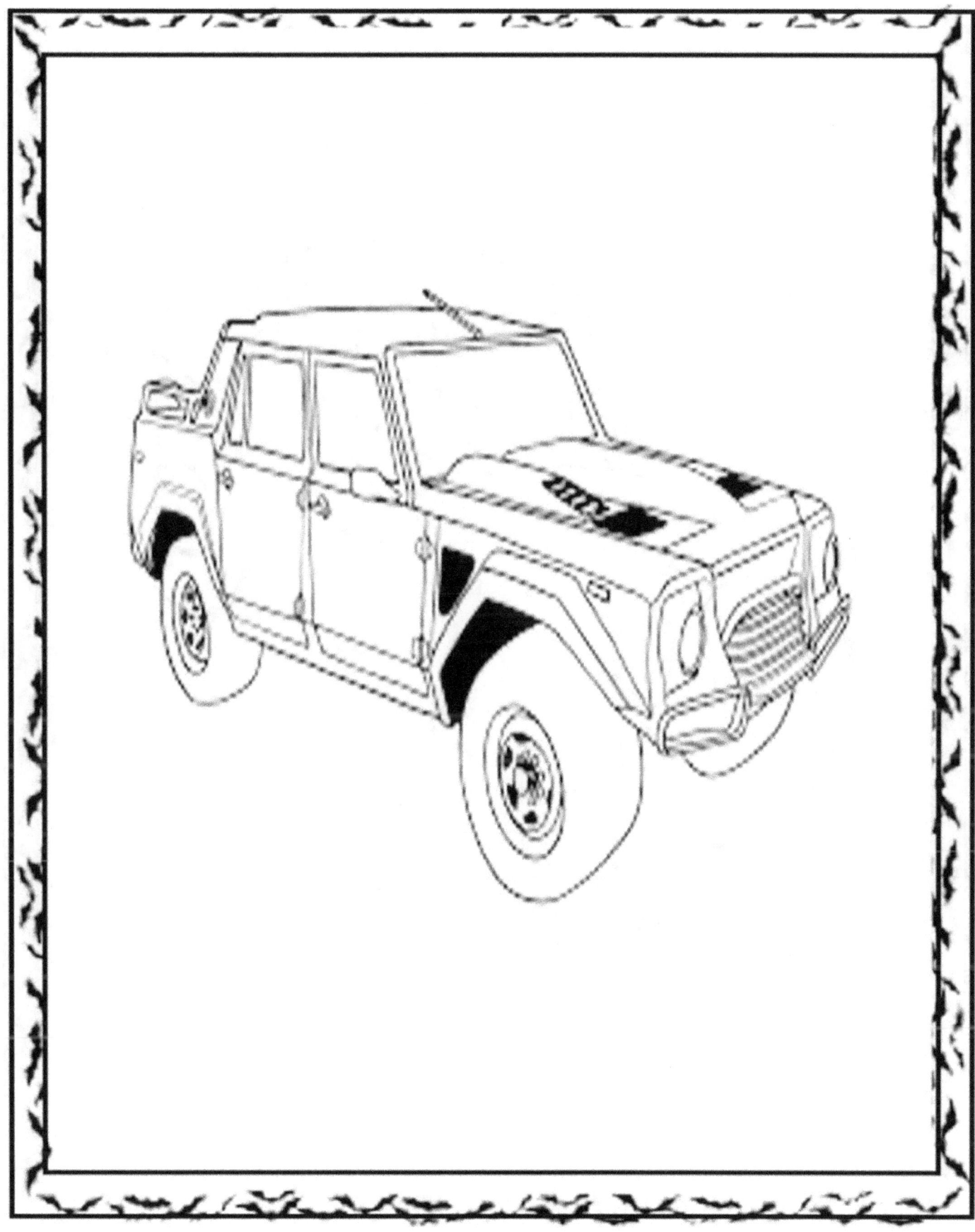

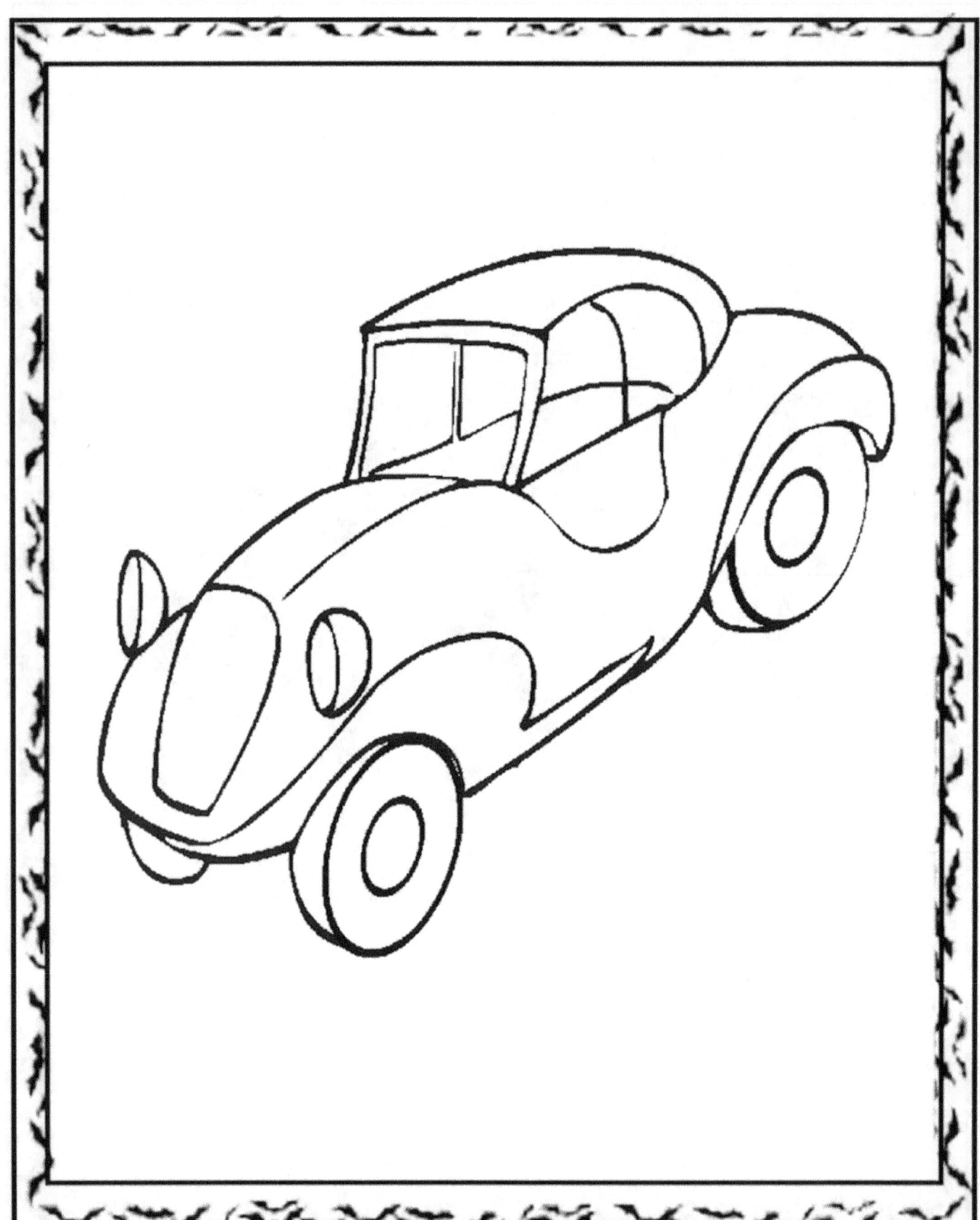

THE END

www.ingramcontent.com/pod-product-compliance
Lightning Source LLC
Chambersburg PA
CBHW080631180526
45168CB00007B/3128